THE WORLD HERITAGE

THE MUGHAL EMPIRE

CHILDRENS PRESS®
CHICAGO

Table of Contents

Library of Congress Cataloging-in-Publication Data
Cervera, Isabel.
  [Imperio Mogol. English]
  The Mughal Empire / by Isabel Cervera.
    p.   cm. —(The World heritage)
  Includes index.
  ISBN 0-516-08392-9
  1. Mughal Empire—History—Juvenile literature. I. Title. II. Series.
  DS461.C3713 1994
  954—dc20   94-16115
                                                      CIP
                                                       AC

El imperio Mogol: © INCAFO S.A./Ediciones S.M./UNESCO 1990
The Mughal Empire: © Childrens Press, Inc./UNESCO 1994

ISBN (UNESCO) 92-3-102681-X
ISBN (Childrens Press) 0-516-08392-9

The Mughal Empire

Beginning in the eighth century A.D., *various Muslim warriors from Central Asia led invasions into India. From the eleventh through the sixteenth centuries, more and more of India came under the control of independent Muslim sultans. Persian was the language of their courts, their government, and fine literature. While Hindu had been India's major religion, the Muslim rulers spread their religion of Islam throughout the subcontinent.*

In the sixteenth century, there arose a Central Asian warrior named Zahir ud-din. He was nicknamed Babur, the Persian word for "panther." Babur tried to take over Fergana, in present-day Uzbekistan, but failed three times. Next, he turned his sights toward India. In 1526 he conquered the sultanate of Delhi after a famous battle at Panipat. The empire he set up in India is known as the Mughal Empire. "Mughal" is simply the Persian word for "Mongol."

The Mughals governed India for over three hundred years. Like their predecessors, they patronized the spread of Persian culture. They also tried to bring Hindus and Muslims together in a unified Indian state. A unique style of art and architecture—called Indo-Islamic—rose out of this cultural blend.

The most outstanding Mughal emperors were Babur (ruled 1526-30), Humayun (1530-1540 and 1554-1556), Akbar (1556-1605), Jahangir (1605-1627), Shah Jahan (1627-1658), and Aurangzeb (1658-1707).

Akbar and Shah Jahan built the greatest works of Indo-Islamic architecture: the Red Fort of Agra, Fatehpur Sikri, the Shalimar Gardens and Fortress of Lahore, and the Taj Mahal.

A Fort of Stone Masonry
The Red Fort of Agra is one of the finest achievements of Indo-Islamic art. It is a solid fortress, surrounded by the sturdy wall shown in the photo. The double wall has a perimeter of a mile and a half (two and one-half kilometers). Like most of the beautiful buildings around it, it was constructed of red sandstone.

5

The Mughal Empire in India

Babur, the founder of the Mughal Empire, had a proud ancestry. He was a descendant of two legendary figures—the Turkish conqueror Timur (Tamerlane) and the Mongol conqueror Genghis Khan. Thus Babur and his successors believed themselves to have the proper "blood" to rule an empire.

Babur was succeeded on the throne by his son Humayun, who ruled during two periods: from 1530 to 1540 and from 1554 to 1556. Humayun's reign was somewhat unstable. A rebel governor defeated him, forcing him into exile in Persia. He returned to rule again for a short time. During the reign of Akbar, Humayun's son, the empire began to be a major political and cultural power.

Akbar ascended the throne when he was barely thirteen years old. The empire at that time was in disarray socially and militarily. Akbar was merely the chief of a foreign minority group—the Muslims. But he turned out to be a shrewd man and an outstanding military leader. During his reign he succeeded in subduing the independent Muslim sultans of the northern third of India. He also created a solid governing framework, thus laying the foundation for the empire's future glory.

Akbar was not occupied solely with the military matters. He was also concerned about the empire's native majority, the Hindus. India's religious diversity often made it difficult for the people to live and work together peacefully. Akbar was interested in all of India's religions, though.

Mughal Expansion
The Mughals occupied a wide territory, where they constructed many outstanding buildings. The buildings shown on the map have been designated World Heritage sites by UNESCO. The upper photo shows the facade of one of the many pavilions of the Fort of Agra. On the left is the North Gate of the Great Mosque and the tombs of the descendants of Salim Chishti in Fatehpur Sikri.

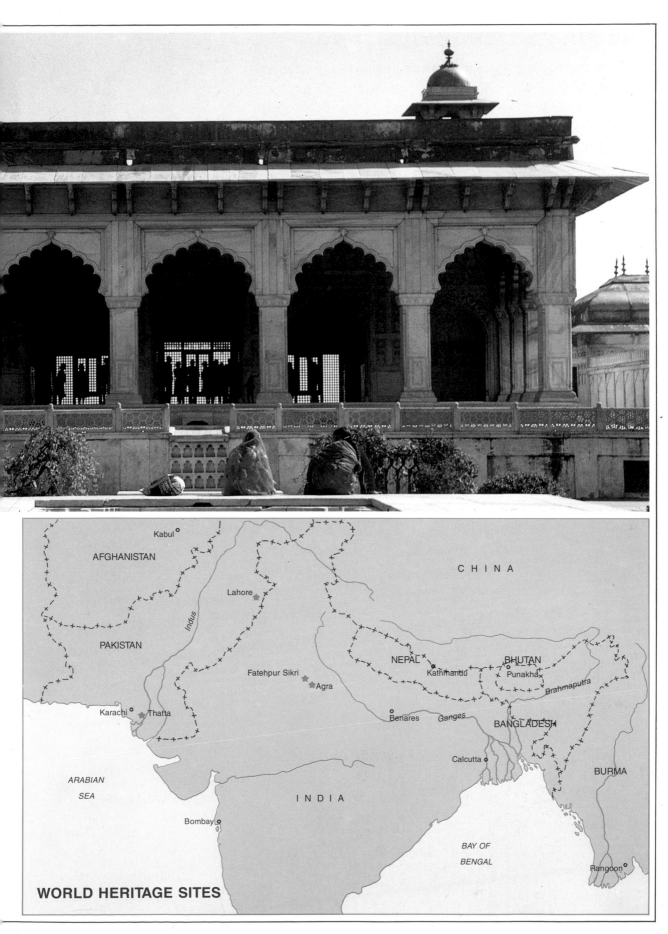

WORLD HERITAGE SITES

Akbar did not discriminate according to social status (caste) or religion. Anyone with talent was given opportunities. He brought into his administration many Hindus who served on equal terms with Muslims. He also eliminated the tax that non-Muslims had to pay. Akbar's taste for cultural unity can be seen in the Indo-Islamic art in Fatehpur Sikri and Agra, cities that arose during the Mughal Empire.

Akbar had many wives, some Hindu and some Muslim. It was a Hindu princess who was the mother of his heir and successor, Jahangir (1605-1627). Jahangir expanded the empire he inherited. His autobiography and the development of miniature painting are two important legacies of his reign. This was a time of peace and prosperity, giving rise to splendid artistic creations.

The next emperor was Shah Jahan, who built the Taj Mahal. During his reign, there were many power struggles within the ruling family. When the country was finally at peace, he built great works of architecture: the Taj Mahal, the interior of the Fort of Agra, and the Shalimar Gardens of Lahore. In these great works, Indo-Islamic art reached its high point.

Aurangzeb (1658-1707) took the throne after a terrible civil war. This struggle led to his father's imprisonment and the deaths of his brothers, son, and nephew. Once established on the throne, Aurangzeb was a firm and effective emperor. When he died, the empire was greater than it had been when he came to power. Aurangzeb was the last of the great Mughals. Eight more emperors followed him over the next fifty-two years. Then, in 1759, the British began their conquest of India. Their triumph was complete in 1877, when the British Queen Victoria was proclaimed Empress of India.

Palaces of Eternal Repose
Mughal tradition often placed great importance on the construction of elaborate tombs for emperors. Other great leaders in the empire had splendid mausoleums, too. Shaikh Salim Chishti's mausoleum *(opposite page, top)* is at the heart of the mosque built in the city of Fatehpur Sikri. The mausoleum in the lower photo stands at the foot of the Makli Hills in the Pakistani city of Thatta.

Decorative Inscription
In the construction of the Taj Mahal, great attention was paid to detail. The beautiful inscriptions on the building's rear door *(left)* are an example of this care.

Indo-Islamic Art

Constant contact between Hindu and Muslim cultures gave rise to a powerful and original new style, most notable in the Mughal period—Indo-Islamic art. By the sixteenth century, the new style was well established. It blended architectural and decorative features of both traditions.

After Humayun's forced stay in Persia, he brought Persian architects and craftsmen with him. This brought new elements to the building style, too. For example, rather flat domes gave way to the Persian-style "onion" domes.

Mughal palaces typically had large halls for audiences. There were separate spaces for public audiences *(Diwan-i-Am)* and for private meetings *(Diwan-i-Khas)*.

Native craftspeople decorated the buildings, carving the window lattices, arches, columns, and doors. Elements of nature—such as flowers and curling vines—were interlaced with inscriptions from the Muslim holy book, the Koran.

This blending of architecture and nature can also be seen in the gardens and fountains. Both were derived from Persian traditions. Kiosks, pavilions, and small gazebos were typically scattered throughout the gardens.

The Shalimar Gardens
The beautiful Shalimar Gardens, in Lahore, cover an area of 50 acres (20 hectares). Serving for many years as a place of recreation for the royal family, they are divided by canals and flowerbeds in the Islamic tradition.

Mosques always faced toward the Muslim holy city of Mecca. They had a typical Persian structure: a square design with an interior courtyard surrounded by a gallery of archways. It contained certain basic elements: the *mihrab* (prayer niche), the *minbar* (pulpit), and minarets (slender towers) at the corners.

Like the palaces, the mosques used such materials as white marble and local red sandstone. They had many doors, balconies, arches with many lobes, and *chhatri,* or small gazebos. Columns were crowned with capitals in the form of lotus blossoms.

During these years, such emperors as Babur, Akbar, and Jahangir followed one of the richest Persian traditions: that of miniature painting. The miniature was used to illustrate beautiful epic tales written in Turkish or Persian.

Humayun introduced Persian traditions, and his son Akbar encouraged the blending of Persian and Indian cultures. Their successors Jahangir and Shah Jahan supported the new style, thus assuring its success.

Timeline of Mughal History

1483 Babur is born in Fergana.
1519 Babur's first military campaign against the Sultanate of Delhi.
1526 Battle of Panipat. Babur conquers Delhi.
1530 Babur dies. His son Humayun succeeds him.
1539 Sher Shan founds the Southern Afghan Dynasty in Delhi, driving Humayun into exile in Persia.
1555 Humayun reconquers Delhi.
1556 Humayun dies. His son Akbar inherits the throne.
1564 Akbar eliminates special tax paid by non-Muslims.
1571 The city of Fatehpur Sikri is founded.
1580 The Jesuits first visit the Mughal court.
1600 The East India Company is founded in England.
1605 Akbar dies. His son Jahangir succeeds him.
1627 Jahangir dies and Shah Jahan takes the throne.
1631 Construction of the Taj Mahal begins.
1658 Aurangzeb deposes Shah Jahan.
1666 Shah Jahan dies.
1679 Taxes are once again levied on citizens who are not Muslims.
1707 Aurangzeb dies.
1773 The British Parliament passes the Regulation Act for India.
1857 The British exile the last Mughal, Bahadur Shah II, after his involvement in the Indian Mutiny.

A New Art Form Is Born from Two

Indo-Islamic art rose from the blending of two unique architectural styles: the Islamic and the Hindu. From the Islamic tradition came the mosque with its characteristic *mihrab, minbar,* and minarets. Hindu tradition incorporated nature into art and used such materials as red sandstone and white marble. In the upper photo is the splendid gate that leads to the interior of the Taj Mahal. Below, on the left, is the balcony of one of the palaces of Agra. On the right is the Audience Hall in the Lahore Fort.

The City of Victory

Fatehpur Sikri, the "City of Victory," is Akbar's master work. The emperor himself designed the city in 1571 and later directed its construction. In Fatehpur Sikri, Akbar achieved his highest ideal: to blend the traditions of Hindus and Persian Muslims into one Indo-Islamic art and culture. Among the city's numerous monuments, the *Diwan-i-Khas*, shown in the photo, is outstanding. Private audiences with the emperor took place there.

Fatehpur Sikri

In 1571, the great Mughal emperor Akbar ordered a new city to be built: Fatehpur Sikri. In part, the city was built in honor of the Muslim mystic Shaikh Salim Chishti. He had prophesied the birth of Akbar's first son, Jahangir. The emperor had the city built on the very spot where the sage lived. The city was also constructed to celebrate Akbar's conquest of Ahmadabad in Gujarat. Its name means "City of Victory."

Building Fatehpur Sikri was not easy. It was necessary to level a hilltop and create an artificial lake, the city's source of water and recreation.

Like an artist, Akbar planned his work and personally supervised its construction. The city is a faithful reflection of Akbar's highest ideals: to blend Persian and Indian traditions in an Indo-Islamic art and culture.

The Short-Lived City
Unfortunately, Fatehpur Sikri had a brief lifespan as capital of the Mughal Empire. The underground streams that supplied its lake changed course. The water receded, making the city uninhabitable. In 1585 Emperor Akbar was forced to return to Agra. Fatehpur Sikri became a dead city. The upper photo is a view of the *Diwan-i-Am,* where the emperor met with public officials. At the left is the Jama Mosque of Fatehpur Sikri, one of the largest in India. At the lower right is the Gate of Victory, also belonging to the mosque.

17

Built of red sandstone, Fatehpur Sikri was surrounded by a wall with seven gates. In the center were the palace complex and the Jama mosque. The palace's public audience room was a broad courtyard with the throne at one end. The private meeting area was surrounded by a balcony and had a small Hindu temple.

The private section of the palace was made up of several buildings: the House of the Turkish Sultana, the House of Mariam, the Khas Mahal, and the mosque. They feature the finest Indo-Islamic ornamentation in their paintings, sculptures, and rich inlays of stone. Besides these buildings, there is the tomb of Shaikh Salim Chishti, which Akbar's son later covered with marble panels.

Fatehpur Sikri was Akbar's retreat for pleasure and relaxation. But it did not serve as the empire's capital for long. The underground streams that fed the lake changed course. As the water dwindled, the city became uninhabitable. Akbar was forced to abandon it and return to Agra. Fatehpur Sikri became a dead city.

The Pointed Arch

The pointed arch is used extensively in Indo-Islamic art, as well as in Islamic architecture in general. Also popular was ornamentation with arabesques—intricate designs with flowers, vines, fruit, and leaves. In the photos at the right are two examples of the use of the pointed arch. *Top:* The inner court of the Great Mosque of Fatehpur. Here classes were taught in the city's Koranic school. *Bottom:* Arcades from the Fort of Lahore. Both buildings are constructed of red sandstone.

The Mansion of Happiness

The Shalimar Gardens, known also as "The Mansion of Happiness," were built by order of Emperor Shah Jahan in 1631. Divided into three terraces, the gardens have more than 450 fountains and waterfalls.

The Fortress of Lahore and the Shalimar Gardens

At Lahore, capital of the Punjab region in present-day Pakistan, the Mughals made their first inroads into India. The Fortress of Lahore stood as a symbol of Mughal military power. However, it was not entirely a Mughal creation. The conquerors simply took over a fort that was already standing. The emperor Akbar then rebuilt it. He made it larger and stronger, replacing clay walls with more solid walls of brick masonry. Akbar's son, Jahangir, continued his father's work and decorated the fort in the Indo-Islamic style. He combined features of Persian art— the horseshoe arch, the square floor plan, and a taste for the monumental—with traditional Indian building materials, marble and red sandstone. In the seventeenth century, Shah Jahan covered the buildings with white marble.

The fort is divided into two distinct sections: an administrative area for royal audiences and a private section. The administrative area is subdivided further. The *Diwan-i-Am* was a place for audiences with lower officers of the government and for the administration of justice. The *Diwan-i-Khas* served the same purposes, but it was reserved for the highest-ranking nobles and merchants. Of these two buildings, only the first remains today.

Monuments Within a Fort
The Fortress of Lahore stood long before the Mughal conquest, but the emperors strengthened and enlarged it. The enclosure contains twenty-one monuments, surrounded by a wide, fortified wall. These photos show three views of the fort. *Opposite page, top:* One of the most spectacular gates. *Opposite page, bottom:* The forest of columns of the *Diwan-i-Am. Left:* A general view of the fort.

Arches on three sides opened to a garden, so that the garden became part of the room itself. In the fourth wall of the enclosure was a balcony, from which the emperor listened to the petitions of his subjects.

In the private section of the palace-fort, the most outstanding feature is the Palace of Mirrors. Built by Shah Jahan for his favorite consort, it is on the fort's north side. The palace's living quarters are topped with cupolas, and the walls are adorned with thousands of small mirrors.

The Naulakha Pavilion, beside the Palace of Mirrors, is unique because it is built entirely of marble. Its simple geometric patterns are very beautiful.

The garden was one of the Persian world's greatest contributions to India. Members of the royal family used the garden as a place for pleasure and relaxation. Its harmonious decoration contained a pleasant blend of architectural elements: kiosks and shaded terraces, fountains, waterfalls, and a wealth of vegetation.

The Shalimar Garden of Lahore was created by the emperor Shah Jahan in the seventeenth century. It is the finest Mughal garden preserved in India. Its buildings are made of Shah Jahan's favorite material: white marble. It contrasts sharply with the red sandstone wall, interrupted by small decorative kiosks. The garden is divided by canals and flowerbeds, following the Persian tradition of *Chahar Bagh*, or "Fourfold Garden."

On the Banks of the Yamuna River
In Agra, on the western bank of the Yamuna River, the emperor Akbar constructed some five hundred buildings. Only a few of them are still standing today. Those that remain were built between 1637 and 1655 during the reign of Shah Jahan. In the upper photo is the facade of one of the fort's entrance gates. Below is the Garden of Grapes, home of the imperial harem.

Special Terms

caste: Hindu social division, based on the concept of purity. There are four castes: brahmans (priests), chatryas (warrior nobles), vaishyas (merchants), and shudras (farmers).

chahar bagh: Literally means "fourfold garden." The canals in such a garden allude to the rivers in the Islamic Paradise.

chhatri: Kiosk or pavilion topped by a cupola. Typical feature of Hindu architecture.

diwan: Very deep, monumental arched portico. Used for public and private audiences.

Koran: (or Qur'an) Sacred book of Islam, believed to be the word of God.

multilobed arch: Arch made up of several small arches.

necropolis: Very large cemetery with many tombs and mausoleums.

sultanate: Government under a sultan or an Islamic prince or governor.

The Red Fort of Agra

The city of Agra was one of the capitals of the Mughal Empire. There, in 1565, the emperor Akbar began to construct a fort on the banks of the Yamuna River. The fort of Agra reflects Akbar's varied tastes and his belief in blending India's cultures. The structure is more than just a fort. Within its walls is a cluster of administrative buildings, small palaces, and private living quarters. The walls have a perimeter of a mile and a half (two and one-half kilometers). There are two entrances to the fort. The more exceptional one is the Delhi Gate. It has two octagonal towers and a vaulted entrance.

Most of the buildings were built of red sandstone (hence the name Red Fort), with inlays of white marble. The interior walls of the two-story buildings were once covered with gold leaf and multicolored paintings. Little remains of the original buildings except the Palace of Jahangir (1570).

The Book of Babur

In miniature painting, we can see the Mughal powers of observation and description and the Hindu appreciation of nature. Babur followed the tradition of illustrating books, and he set up workshops at his court with Persian and Hindu artists. The *Baburnamah,* or the Book of Babur, was written by the emperor and illustrated by his grandson Akbar. In it the author describes his military campaigns and the relationships between various members of his family. He also makes a series of observations about Turkestan, Afghanistan, and Hindustan. When writing of Hindustan he speaks of the caste system, as well as the land's geography, history, method of counting and measuring time, and its plants and animals.

Babur's memoirs, which began when the author was twelve, are written in Turkish. In 1559 Akbar had them translated into Persian and ordered various illustrations. Today museums preserve four versions from Akbar's time. The miniature paintings illustrate the text and contain as much detail as the literary descriptions.

To create a miniature, the basic design was sketched out first. Then the human figures were painted, then the animals, and finally the background. Brilliant colors—such as "Persian blue"—were derived from minerals, insects, and animals. The pictures were completed with gold, silver, and copper to reflect the luxury of the Mughal court. These miniatures show an excellent understanding of perspective.

Many artists were involved in completing a single work. As many as forty artists worked on the Book of Babur, though the emperor himself directed their efforts. In addition to the *Baburnamah,* many other Indo-Mughal miniatures still survive. By studying them, we can learn much about the lives and customs of these people.

From the Times of Akbar
The Palace of Jahangir is the only important construction from Akbar's era that survives in the Red Fort of Agra. It is a red sandstone palace, square in design. Unfortunately, the multicolored pictures that once adorned its walls have disappeared. The upper photo is an exterior view of the fortress wall. The lower photo shows the fort's main facade.

Shah Jahan, Akbar's grandson, demolished the buildings within the fort and rebuilt them, following principles of Persian art. One of its main features was the use of white marble as a construction material.

Among Shah Jahan's many constructions, the most striking is the Khas Mahal. This is a private palace consisting of three pavilions. The central pavilion is dominated by a fountain, with richly decorated niches and walls. Also remarkable are the Shish Mahal, or Palace of Mirrors, designed as a bathhouse; and the Muthamman Burj, residence of the favorite consort, with inlays of hard stones and a central fountain on the main floor.

Besides the buildings intended for the court, Shah Jahan built two small mosques of white marble. The Moti Masjid, or Pearl Mosque, stands on a sandstone platform. Its prayer chamber has a rich facade, composed of seven multilobed arches.

The Taj Mahal

The Taj Mahal, or "Crown of the Court," was built by the emperor Shah Jahan between 1631 and 1648. It is a group of funerary buildings surrounding the mausoleum of Arjamand Banu, the emperor's favorite wife. The woman, known also by the title Mumtaz Mahal, meaning "Famous in the Court," died in 1630 after giving birth to her fourteenth child.

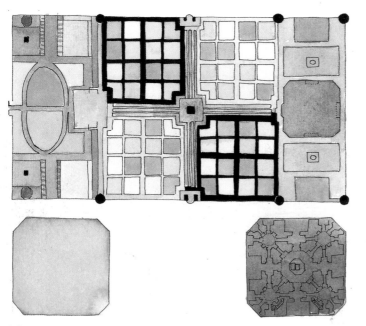

One feature sets the Taj Mahal apart from other Mughal mausoleums of its time. It stands at the northern end of an enclosure, rather than at the center. Some 20,000 workers took part in its construction (1631-1648), directed by Ustad Ahmad Lahori, Emperor Shah Jahan's official architect. The mausoleum's cupola reaches 184 feet (56 meters) in height. The photo shows the mausoleum in its full splendor, completed in Makrana marble. The funerary chamber contains the remains of Shah Jahan and his favorite wife, Mumtaz Mahal.

The Design of the Taj Mahal
The mausoleum of the Taj Mahal, octagonal in design, occupies the northern end of a large rectangle. In the center of the rectangle is a square garden divided by a shallow fountain. At the southern end, the entrance gate opens on a broad quadrangle surrounded by arcades.

Shah Jahan was a master at blending Persian and Indian traditions. He chose a beautiful location on the banks of the Yamuna River. The Taj Mahal is the most outstanding of an elegant group of buildings.

The finest materials and methods were used to build the Taj Mahal: translucent marble from Makrana, semiprecious stones, and exquisite motifs and decorative techniques. Its octagonal design comes from the Persian tradition of the Eight Paradises. The building stands upon a terrace of red sandstone, topped with four minarets. At the center of the platform stands the mausoleum, with a great pointed arch in the center. The interior of the funerary chamber has the same octagonal structure as the outer walls. The building is crowned by an immense, round cupola. This entire structure is made of Makrana marble. Decorations on the inside and outside combine arabesques and floral patterns with geometric and linear designs in semiprecious stones. Bas-reliefs and inscriptions from the Koran garnish the interior. Gardens spread before the mausoleum, with a fountain that reflects the building. In the Persian style, these gardens are divided by canals and flowerbeds.

This building, plus two red sandstone buildings intended as a mosque and a guest house, can be admired from the opposite bank of the Yamuna River. Here Shah Jahan had planned to build his own mausoleum of black marble. But his son Aurangzeb deposed him some years before he died, so he never had the chance to build it. Aurangzeb had no desire to spend the money to build his father a tomb. Instead, he buried Shah Jahan next to the shah's wife.

The Emperor's Impossible Dream

The platform that supports the Taj Mahal's mausoleum (right) is flanked by four identical minarets. Each stands 135 feet (41 meters) high and is crowned by a kiosk topped with a cupola. The photo at the left shows the interior of the funerary chamber, the final resting place of the imperial couple. Shah Jahan actually planned to build a second mausoleum, this one of black marble, on the river's opposite bank. But his son deposed him before he had a chance to build it. Shah Jahan was buried beside his wife.

Historic Monuments of Thatta

The Necropolis of Thatta is located in the province of Sind, in present-day Pakistan. Thatta was the capital of Lower Sind from the middle of the fifteenth to the middle of the eighteenth century. Several dynasties ruled during this era: the Sammah, Argun, Traklan, and Mughal.

The most important necropolis of Thatta covers about 5.8 square miles (15 square kilometers). Here are found examples of construction from several dynasties. These ruins can be classified according to two types: carved stone monuments, and brick monuments decorated with enameled tiles.

In Thatta the Mughal emperors built monuments of the second type. They combined local traditions with the grandness and ornamentation of Indo-Islamic art. The most commonly used material was the red sandy stone of Thatta, instead of the marble they used elsewhere in India.

The tombs are hexagonal in design, crowned with a cupola. A woman's tomb was marked with a jewel, and a man's tomb bore a mounted soldier. One of the most original tombs is that of Isa Khan Tarkhan, "the Young," with its highly decorative bas-relief.

Thatta's mosques represent another type of building. One of them was constructed by the emperor Shah Jahan in 1647 and completed by his son Aurangzeb in 1658. It is a brick structure, decorated with the finest blue Thatta tiles. It features a group of symmetrical stucco arches painted with floral patterns.

Because such fragile materials were used, most of these structures have been seriously damaged. Unfortunately, little remains today of the once-splendid city of Thatta.

Landmarks of Indo-Islamic Art
The Mughals endowed Indo-Islamic art with great importance and beauty. UNESCO has designated many of these architectural treasures as World Heritage sites. Shown at the right are a general view of the Fort of Lahore, the mausoleum of the Taj Mahal, elephants decorating the wall of the Fort of Agra, and the Gate of Victory at Fatehpur Sikri. In the photo at the left is a tomb in the necropolis of Thatta.

These Sites Are Part of the World Heritage

Fatehpur Sikri (India): The emperor Akbar ordered the "City of Victory" to be built in 1571 to commemorate his military victories and the birth of his first son. An example of Indo-Islamic architecture, it was abandoned for lack of water in 1586.

The Fortress of Lahore and the Shalimar Gardens (Pakistan): Military and civil works in which all of the great Mughal emperors took part, from Akbar to Shah Jahan, in the sixteenth and seventeenth centuries. Outstanding among them are the two Audience Chambers, the Palace of Mirrors, and the Naulakha Pavilion. The Shalimar Gardens, created by Shah Jahan, maintained the Persian tradition of canals and flowerbeds.

The Red Fort of Agra (India): Built by Akbar in 1565 with a perimeter of a mile and a half (two and one-half kilometers). The Delhi Gate, the Palace of Jahangir, the Audience Chambers, and the Pearl Mosque are its most representative buildings.

Taj Mahal (India): Funerary monument in the city of Agra. It was built between 1631 and 1648 by Shah Jahan in memory of his wife, Mumtaz Mahal. Built of white marble, it is considered one of the finest architectural works in history.

Historic Monuments of Thatta (Pakistan): Thatta, in the province of Sind, has a great necropolis that covers 5.8 square miles (15 square kilometers). There stand various types of funerary and religious monuments built between the fifteenth and eighteenth centuries. They reflect the local tradition of blue tile and the Mughal enthusiasm for monuments.

Glossary

administrative: having to do with governing or managing public affairs

arabesque: a decorative pattern using intricate flower, leaf, and vine designs

consort: a companion

cupola: a circular structure that forms a rounded ceiling or sits on top of a roof

exile: a forced removal from one's country or home

facade: the front of a building

gazebo: a small structure with a roof and open sides

hexagonal: six-sided

inscription: a piece of writing or engraving

kiosk: a small structure whose sides are partly or completely open

legacy: something from the past left behind for later generations

masonry: brickwork or stonework

mausoleum: a large tomb; a building where people's remains are buried

minaret: a tall tower attached to a mosque, from which a crier calls people to prayer

mosque: a Muslim house of worship

motif: a repeated design or theme in a piece of art

necropolis: a large cemetery, especially one in an ancient city

octagonal: eight-sided

pavilion: a light, decorative structure in a garden or park, used for recreation or entertainment

perimeter: the outside boundary

predecessor: one who lived or reigned before someone

shrewd: crafty and wise

stucco: a type of cement building material

subcontinent: a vast piece of land that is part of a continent

sultan: a Muslim ruler

symmetrical: balanced in design, with one side being a reflection of the other

translucent: letting light shine through

vaulted: arched; curved; rounded

Index

Page numbers in boldface type indicate illustrations.

Titles in the World Heritage Series

Photo Credits

Front Cover: D. Azqueta Bernar/Incafo; p. 3: L. Ruiz Pastor/Incafo; p. 5:
D. Azqueta/Incafo; p. 6: L. R. Pastor/Incafo; p. 7: D. Azqueta/Incafo;
p. 8: D. Azqueta/Incafo; p. 9: L. R. Pastor/Incafo, R. Denis; p. 10: L. R.
Pastor/Incafo; p. 11: D. Azqueta/Incafo; p. 13: D. Azqueta/Incafo;
pp. 13-21: L. R. Pastor/Incafo; pp. 23-29: D. Azqueta/Incafo; p. 30:
R. Denis; p. 31: L. R. Pastor/Incafo, D. Azqueta/Incafo, L. R.
Pastor/Incafo, D. Azqueta/Incafo; back cover: L. R. Pastor/Incafo,
J. Gomez Cano/Incafo.

Project Editor, Childrens Press: Ann Heinrichs
Original Text: Isabel Cervera
Subject Consultant: Dr. Gregory C. Kozlowski
Translator: Deborah Kent
Design: Alberto Caffaratto
Cartography: Modesto Arregui
Phototypesetting: Publishers Typesetters Inc.

UNESCO's World Heritage

The United Nations Educational, Scientific, and Cultural Organization (UNESCO) was founded in 1946. Its purpose is to contribute to world peace by promoting cooperation among nations through education, science, and culture. UNESCO believes that such cooperation leads to universal respect for justice, for the rule of law, and for the basic human rights of all people.

UNESCO's many activities include, for example, combatting illiteracy, developing water resources, educating people on the environment, and promoting human rights.

In 1972, UNESCO established its World Heritage Convention. With members from over 100 nations, this international body works to protect cultural and natural wonders throughout the world. These include significant monuments, archaeological sites, geological formations, and natural landscapes. Such treasures, the Convention believes, are part of a World Heritage that belongs to all people. Thus, their preservation is important to us all.

Specialists on the World Heritage Committee have targeted over 300 sites for preservation. Through technical and financial aid, the international community restores, protects, and preserves these sites for future generations.

Volumes in the *World Heritage* series feature spectacular color photographs of various World Heritage sites and explain their historical, cultural, and scientific importance.